BEHIND THE PLATE

AMERICAN LEAGUE EAST

THE BALTIMORE ORIOLES, THE BOSTON RED SOX, THE NEW YORK YANKEES, THE TAMPA BAY DEVIL RAYS, AND THE TORONTO BLUE JAYS

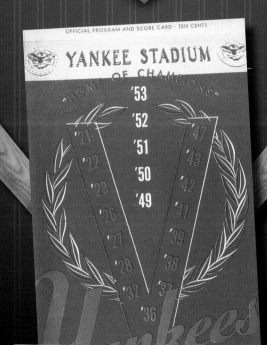

BY JAMES BUCKLEY JR.

American League East: The Baltimore Orioles, the Boston Red Sox, the New York Yankees, the Tampa Bay Devil Rays, and the Toronto Blue Jays

Published in the United States of America by The Child's World®

PO Box 326 • Chanhassen, MN 55317-0326 • 800-599-READ • www.childsworld.com

Acknowledgements:

The Child's World®: Mary Berendes, Publishing Director

Editorial Directions, Inc.: E. Russell Primm, Editorial Director; Matthew Messbarger, Line Editor; Katie Marsico, Assistant Editor; Susan Hindman, Copy Editor; Sarah E. De Capua, Proofreader; Kevin Cunningham, Fact Checker; Tim Griffin/IndexServ, Indexer; James Buckley Jr., Photo Researcher and Selector

The Design Lab: Kathleen Petelinsek, Art Direction and Design; Kari Thornborough, Page Production

Cover:
Derek Jeter

Page one:
old New York
Yankees program

Photos:

Al Bello/Getty: Cover
Bettmann/Corbis: 6, 9, 17, 24, 36
Roberto Borea/AP: 12
Corbis: 7
Mark Duncan/AP: 40
Duomo/Corbis: 21
Getty Images: 35
Jeff Gross/Getty Images: 29
Otto Gruele, Jr./Getty: 41
Harry Howe/Allsport/Getty Images: 37
Hulton Archive: 14
Jed Jacobsohn/Getty: 18
Vince LaForet/Getty: 30
Rob Leiter/Getty Images: 27
Doug Mills/AP: 38
Peter Murphy/AFP/Getty Images: 33
National Baseball Hall of Fame/Getty Images: 23
Doug Pensinger/Getty: 10
Reuters/Corbis: 4
Rucker Archives: 20
Transcendental Graphics: 1, 13

Library of Congress Cataloging-in-Publication Data

Buckley, James, 1963–
   American League East / by James Buckley, Jr.
      p. cm. — (Behind the plate)
   Includes index.
   ISBN 1-59296-359-5 (lib. bdg. : alk. paper) 1. American League of Professional Baseball Clubs—
Juvenile literature. I. Title. II. Series.
   GV875.A15B83 2005
   796.357'64'0973—dc22   2004016733

Table of Contents

Team: Baltimore
Orioles

Founded: 1901

Park: Oriole Park

Park Opened: 1992

Colors: Black and
orange

Team: Boston
Red Sox

Founded: 1901

Park: Fenway Park

Park Opened: 1912

Colors: Red, white,
and blue

The American League (AL) East Division is the
most successful of baseball's six divisions. Its five
teams have won 37 **World Series** titles—far more
than any other division. Of course, it helps that
the New York Yankees are one of those five teams. By
themselves, the Yankees account for 26 championships,
which is almost three times as many as the second-place
St. Louis Cardinals. That National League (NL) Central
team has nine titles.

However, three of the other four teams in the East

The Yankees celebrate their World Series win in 2000.

Division, which was established in its current form in 1994, have also won championships. The Boston Red Sox can point to a century of great baseball. They won the first World Series in 1903 and the 100th in 2004, with four others in between. The Orioles have won three World Series titles—most recently in 1983—since moving to Baltimore in 1954. Though they only joined the major leagues in 1977, the Toronto Blue Jays have two World Series titles, from 1992 through 1993. Only the newest member of the division, the Tampa Bay Devil Rays, has yet to hold the championship trophy.

Amid all these championships, the three oldest teams— Red Sox, Yankees, and Orioles—have produced many of baseball's greatest stars. More than 60 members of the Baseball Hall of Fame have come from the Sox and Yanks alone. The rivalry between the two clubs has been one of sports' most famous and most furious. Even in recent seasons, the fate of the AL **pennant** hinged on a series between the two teams. The Yankees came out on top in 2003, while the Red Sox beat New York in 2004.

Meanwhile, though the Blue Jays and Orioles have faded recently, they have built great **traditions** of base-ball in their home cities. Tampa Bay has some fine models within its own division to look to as it builds its own tradition.

The Baltimore Orioles

When the St. Louis Browns of the NL moved to Baltimore in 1954, they helped the city continue a long tradition of big-league baseball. In the 1890s, the first team known as the Orioles was one of the best in baseball. That team was part of the NL from 1892 until they moved to the new AL in 1901. After the 1902 season, however, the team left Baltimore and moved to New York (later becoming the Yankees).

Baltimore was without a major league team until the Browns arrived in 1954. The Browns franchise brought with it a long history of failure. This new Orioles team set about creating a more impressive record.

By 1960, the Orioles were challenging for the AL pennant. Young third baseman Brooks Robinson was one of the team's stars. Robinson was perhaps the best-

Bob Dillinger

**Brooks Robinson's ability to dive and catch just about any line drive
or grounder made him one of the best defensive players ever.**

fielding third baseman of all time. By the time he
finally retired in 1977, he had set a record for most
years played with one team (23).

Outfielder Frank Robinson (no relation to Brooks)
and first baseman Boog Powell helped provide
offense. Meanwhile, Baltimore was putting together
a pitching staff that would put them over the top.

Perhaps the key to Baltimore's success in the
coming years would be Manager Earl Weaver. A fiery

Orioles teams of the
1890s were led by
third baseman John
McGraw. He would
later become the
famous manager of
the New York Giants.

For the old St. Louis Browns, George Sisler was a huge star. He set a single-season record with 257 hits in 1920. His .420 average in 1922 is one of the highest ever.

leader, he was as well known for yelling at umpires as he was for winning ball games.

In 1966, the Orioles won their first AL pennant—led in part by young pitcher Jim Palmer, who had 15 wins. (In the next 12 years, Palmer, a future Hall of Famer, would win more than 200 games.) The O's, as they are sometimes called, took on the Dodgers in the World Series. Baltimore pitchers allowed only two runs in four games, and the O's were world champs.

In 1969, baseball divided its two leagues into divisions. Baltimore won the very first AL East title. They defeated the Minnesota Twins of the AL West in the first AL Championship Series (ALCS). Though the O's lost to the Mets in the World Series, their 1969 team was one of the best ever, setting a club record with 109 wins.

During the 1970s, an Orioles fan named Wild Bill Hagy became famous for standing atop the team dugout and spelling out O-R-I-O-L-E-S with his body while fans chanted.

In 1970, the O's continued their hot streak. Pitchers Mike Cuellar, Dave McNally, and Palmer each won more than 20 games. In the World Series, Baltimore defeated Cincinnati. Brooks Robinson made several spectacular defensive plays and was named Most Valuable Player (MVP).

In the 1970s, the Orioles won four more division titles (1971, '73, '74, and '79), but lost the World Series twice (1971 and '79). The 1979 series featured

Jim Palmer was one of baseball's best pitchers in the 1960s and 1970s.

The Orioles home ballpark at Camden Yards is one of the most beautiful in baseball.

In 1988, the Orioles set a record they wished they hadn't. They lost 21 games in a row to start the season.

an exciting climax, and the O's fell to the Pirates in seven games.

In 1983, the Orioles won it all again, this time led by a young shortstop named Cal Ripken Jr. Cal's father had been a coach and manager for the Orioles for many years. The younger Ripken was tall for a shortstop and—unlike most other shortstops—was a great hitter and runs-batted-in (RBI) man. His combination of hitting and fielding skills helped him win the 1983 AL MVP award, an honor he would earn again in 1991.

In 1992, big news in Baltimore baseball occurred when a new ballpark opened. Oriole Park at Camden Yards was the first of a string of new ballparks, and remains one of the best. Fans flocked to see the new baseball palace with its famous brick exterior. Everyone from players to reporters to umpires praised the new field.

In 1995, the sure and steady Ripken excited the sports world when—in his 15th season—he broke a record many thought would never be broken. The great Yankees first baseman Lou Gehrig had played in 2,130 straight games from 1926 to 1939. Ripken avoided major injuries and toughed out minor ones to finally crack Gehrig's magic number on September 6, 1995. Millions watched on TV as Baltimore fans gave Ripken a 20-minute standing **ovation.** It was one of baseball's most memorable moments.

Orioles pitchers have won the Cy Young Award six times: Jim Palmer had three, while Mike Cuellar, Mike Flanagan, and Steve Stone each won one.

A batted ball that bounces very high on, or in front of, home plate is known as a Baltimore chop. (The name originally described the hits of Hall of Famer Wee Willie Keeler who played for the city's NL franchise in the late 1800s.)

Frank Robinson won the AL Triple Crown in 1966, leading the league in homers, RBIs, and batting average.

The following year, the team was also great, setting a major league record with 257 homers. Brady Anderson led the way with 50, while Rafael Palmeiro had 39.

The team followed up Ripken's magic with division titles in 1996 and 1997. Unfortunately, the Orioles have had few memorable moments since. They finished in fourth place in the division every year from 1997 to 2003 before rising to third in 2004.

Fans saluted Cal Ripken Jr. after he broke the consecutive-games-played record in 1995.

The Boston Red Sox

Until 2004, the history of the Boston Red Sox (at least since their early days) was one of disappointment. Though perhaps one of baseball's most beloved teams, they were also seemingly one of the most cursed. Through it all, their fans—sometimes known as Red Sox Nation— remained fiercely loyal. Though they almost seem to count on the team failing in the clutch, they come out again each April hoping things will be different this time. Then, in 2004, things were indeed different. The dreams of genera- tions of fans came true and the Red Sox became world champions for the first time in 86 years.

The Red Sox began with a bang and seemed destined for a great life. Born in 1901 as one of the first mem- bers of the new AL, they won the first World Series ever played, in 1903. From 1912 to 1918, they won four of

OFFICIAL PROGRAM AND SCORECARD

19

Red S

HOME OF AMERICAN LEAGUE BASE

seven championships. Among the stars on those early teams were pitchers Cy Young and Joe Wood and outfielders Tris Speaker and Harry Hooper.

Then the roof fell in. Owner Harry Frazee did something that has haunted the team and its fans ever since. He sold left-handed pitcher-outfielder Babe Ruth, who had just hit a record 29 homers in 1919, to the New York Yankees. Ruth went on to dominate baseball. The Red Sox went 86 years without a title. Frazee's selfish act and the Red Sox tradition of near-misses are known today as The Curse of the Bambino, after Ruth's famous nickname. From 1919 to 2003, the team would play in four World Series and lose each one in the seventh game. They would lose two one-game play-offs and twice in the ALCS to the Yankees. In that same period, the Yankees would win 26 world titles.

The greatest player in Red Sox history joined the team in 1939 as a **brash** young rookie. Ted Williams said he had one goal in life. "When I walk down the street," he said then, "I want people to say, 'There goes the greatest hitter who ever lived.'" Many experts think he made that claim come true. In 1941,

Ted Williams, "the Splendid Splinter," worked tirelessly to create a hitting stroke that made him one of the greatest hitters of all time.

The Red Sox were first known as the Americans and later as the Pilgrims and the Somersets. They officially became the Red Sox in 1908.

The late Tom Yawkey owned the team from 1933 to 1976. His initials— and those of his wife, Jean—are shown in Morse code on the left-field scoreboard.

Williams hit .406 and became the last player ever over the magic .400 mark. He would end his career with a .344 average and 521 homers, including one in his final at bat in 1960. Williams led the Sox to only one World Series, which they lost in seven games in 1946 to the Cardinals.

Taking over for Williams in left field in 1961 was another great lefty hitter. Carl "Yaz" Yastrzemski would become the first AL player ever with both 3,000 hits and 400 homers in his career. He tied a record by playing with the same team for 23 years, and no one ever played the **Green Monster** as well as Yaz. In 1967, he led the Red Sox to the World Series while winning the Triple Crown. He was the last player to accomplish that rare feat. Needing to win two games against the Twins to clinch the pennant, Yaz went seven-for-eight, including a homer in the final game.

Again, the Sox lost the World Series in seven games, and again they lost to the Cardinals.

In 1975, the stars aligned again and the Red Sox found themselves in the World Series. At Fenway Park against the Cincinnati Reds in Game 6, Boston won perhaps the most exciting World Series game ever played. They trailed 6–3 going into the

Carl Yastrzemski slugged this home run during the 1967 World Series, but it wasn't enough to help Boston win the title.

eighth inning. A loss would end the season, but pinch hitter Bernie Carbo tied the score with a stunning homer. The game went back and forth in extra innings. Boston had a runner thrown out at home. Boston's Dwight Evans stole a home run from Cincinnati's Joe Morgan. Then came the bottom of the 12th.

Catcher Carlton Fisk stepped up for the Sox as the clock neared midnight. He hit the second pitch high and deep toward the Green Monster in left. Would it stay fair? A famous television shot shows Fisk waving his arms and dancing as he runs up the first base line. It was indeed fair and Boston had won. Fisk's shot remains among baseball's most

In 1975, Fred Lynn became the first player to win Rookie of the Year and MVP in the same season.

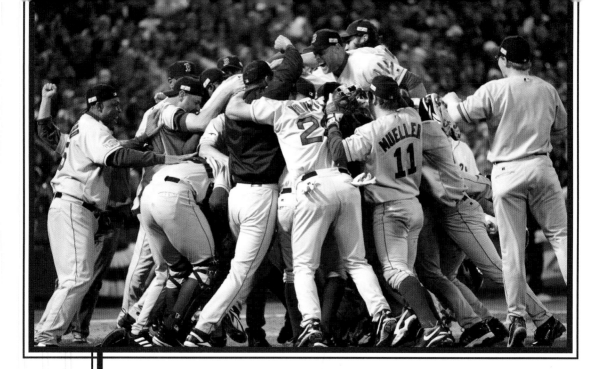

The Red Sox celebrate their stunning 2004 World Series victory with a giant group hug.

In 2003, the Red Sox added special "Monster Seats" atop the green left-field wall. Lucky fans get a great view of the action and are in a perfect spot to catch home run balls.

memorable hits. However, the Curse was in effect and Boston lost Game 7, even though they were ahead at one point.

In 1978, the Sox faced the Yankees—their hated rival—in a one-game playoff for the AL East title. (They had tied during the regular season.) The Yankees' light-hitting shortstop Bucky Dent hit a three-run homer to knock the Red Sox out.

In 1986, the Curse struck again. In Game 6 of the series against the Mets, the Sox were one strike away from winning it all. But Bob Stanley threw a wild pitch that let the tying run score. The Mets won the game when Bill Buckner couldn't handle a ground ball. The Sox lost Game 7, of course.

The Curse struck again most recently in 2003, when Boston blew a three-run lead against the Yankees in Game 7 of the ALCS at Yankee Stadium. New York tied the game in the seventh and then won it on Aaron Boone's Fisk-like homer in the eleventh.

However, the sun shone on Red Sox Nation again in 2004. After winning the AL East **wild-card** spot, Boston beat Anaheim in the Division Series. The Sox lost the first three games of the ALCS to the hated Yankees, but then did something that had never been done in baseball history. Down three games to none, they came back to win four straight and the AL pennant, their first since 1986. The feat stunned and thrilled the baseball world, but for Red Sox fans, the best was yet to come.

In the World Series, they faced the St. Louis Cardinals, winners of 105 games and baseball's most dominant team in 2004. That didn't matter to a pack of easy-going, long-haired "idiots," as the Red Sox players called themselves. Boston won four straight over St. Louis, combining dominating pitching with outstanding offense. Suddenly, it was over. The Red Sox were something that many thought they would never be: World Series champs. Millions of people all over New England knew that the "Curse" was finally lifted.

The Red Sox have retired five uniform numbers: #1, Bobby Doerr; #4, Joe Cronin; #8, Carl Yastrzemski; #9, Ted Williams; and #27, Carlton Fisk.

In Fenway Park's deep center field seating area, there is one red seat amid the green bleacher seats. It marks the spot where a very long home run by Ted Williams landed in 1946.

The New York Yankees

To the frustration of the rest of the AL, the New York Yankees are the most successful pro sports team in the world. No other team in any sport has won as many world championships as the Yankees, who have 26 World Series titles. In baseball, the St. Louis Cardinals are a distant second, with nine series wins. The National Hockey League's Montreal Canadiens have 24 Stanley Cup titles, while the Boston Celtics have 16 National Basketball Association championships. In the National Football League, the Green Bay Packers lead the way with 12 Super Bowl wins. Season after season, the Yankees seem to boast the greatest names and the most complete teams. Playing in historic Yankee Stadium, they have created a tradition of winning that continues to this day.

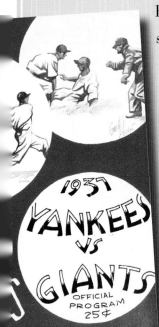

Yankee Stadium, which opened in 1923, holds more than 55,000 fans and is one of baseball's biggest ballparks.

The Yankees' first five decades can be traced through four players: Babe Ruth, Lou Gehrig, Joe DiMaggio, and Mickey Mantle. Other stars contributed, of course, but these players were the centerpieces.

The team got a slow start on its way to greatness. They began play as the New York Highlanders when the Baltimore Orioles franchise moved to New York City in 1903. For almost 20 years, they were nearly

Hall of Fame pitcher Whitey Ford won 10 World Series games for the Yankees— the most ever.

The Yankees have retired 16 uniform numbers—more than any other team. The only single-digit numbers available are #2 and #6 (and Derek Jeter has #6).

While helping New York win 10 championships, catcher Yogi Berra set World Series records for most runs, hits, games played, and RBIs.

invisible. They didn't even have their own field for much of that time, sharing space with the New York Giants in the Polo Grounds.

In 1920, however, baseball changed forever. First, in order to increase offense and fan interest in the game, the owners decided to use a livelier baseball that would travel farther when hit. Second, a young former Red Sox pitcher came to the Yankees in a deal that still haunts the Red Sox. Babe Ruth had helped the Boston team win three World Series as an ace lefty. (An ace is the best pitcher on a team.) Moving to New York—and the outfield—he literally changed the way baseball was played. Prior to Ruth and his stunning home run power, most teams played for one run, using bunts, steals, and other "small ball" tactics. The mighty Bambino proved that slugging wins championships. In 1920, he had 54 homers. Only one other big-league team had as many. In 1921, he hit 59!

Yankee Stadium opened in 1923. It was the largest ballpark ever built and was the first with three decks of seats. Ruth hit a homer in the first game there, and the Yankees won their first World Series. To this day, the place is known as The House That Ruth Built. The Yanks returned to the top in

The slugging duo of Lou Gehrig (left) and Babe Ruth (right)
turned the Yankees into a mighty baseball machine.

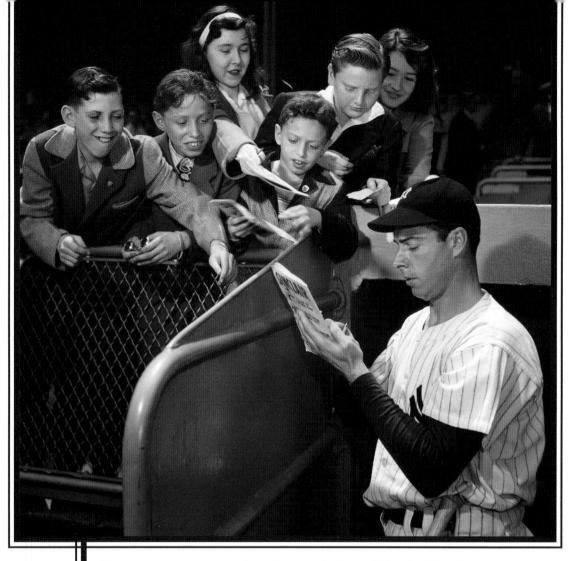

These lucky young fans got an autograph from star Yankees outfielder Joe DiMaggio.

One of the Yankees'
nicknames is the
Bronx Bombers. The
Bronx is the section
of New York City
where they play.

1927 with perhaps the finest baseball team ever put together. Ruth set a record of 60 homers that stood for 34 years.

By then, Ruth had been joined by first baseman Lou Gehrig. If not for Ruth, Gehrig might have been regarded as baseball's greatest slugger. His 184 RBIs in 1931 is still an AL record. He had a stunning eight

seasons with more than 140 RBIs and nine seasons
with 130 or more runs scored. The duo of Ruth
and Gehrig led to World Series wins in 1927, 1928,
and 1932.

After Ruth joined the Boston Braves in 1935,
Gehrig continued to lead the team. From 1936 to
1939, the Yankees won every single World Series. No
other team had ever done that. Gehrig himself put
together another streak: a then-record 2,130 consecutive games played. Sadly, Gehrig had to stop playing
due to a nerve disease that took his life in 1941.
Today, this illness is called **Lou Gehrig's disease.**

Smooth-fielding outfielder Joe DiMaggio joined
the team in 1936. "Joltin' Joe" didn't hit tons of
homers like Ruth and Gehrig, but he was one of
baseball's most consistent hitters. His record streak
of 56 straight games with a hit in 1941 should stand
forever. DiMaggio lost several years of his career due
to service in World War II, but he helped the Yankees
win four more World Series titles. He helped start
another streak that is still a record: the Yanks' five
straight championships from 1949 to 1953.

In 1951, the year DiMaggio retired, a speedy
slugger from Oklahoma picked up the torch. Mickey
Mantle was the greatest **switch-hitter** of all time and

**The Yankees are
one of the few major
league teams that
doesn't put names
on the backs of
players' uniforms.**

**George Steinbrenner
has been the
principal owner
of the team since
1973. Known as The
Boss, Steinbrenner
used to be famous
for frequently
changing managers.**

perhaps one of baseball's fastest runners, until a
knee injury slowed his speed. Mantle cracked 536
lifetime homers and helped the Yanks win seven
series titles from 1951 to 1962.

From then until 1977, the team went through its
only down period. Then another slugging star arrived
to lead the way. Reggie Jackson helped the Yankees
win the 1977 World Series by hitting three homers
on three pitches in the deciding Game 6. The
Yanks repeated in 1978, but were mostly quiet in
the 1980s. A star for them in those years was first
baseman Don Mattingly, the 1985 AL MVP.

In 1995, the team started its current run of
success by winning the AL East Championship. They
won the 1996 World Series thanks in part to ace
relief pitcher John Wetteland. **Closer** Mariano Rivera
took over for Wetteland in 1997 and proved to be a
key to the team's winning titles from 1998 to 2000.

Along with Rivera, shortstop Derek Jeter has
been vital to the team's success. The Yankees'
captain is a clutch hitter with a .306 batting average
in **postseason** play. A very talented group of starting
pitchers has also helped the Yanks in recent
seasons, including players such as Mike Mussina,
Andy Pettite, David Wells, and future Hall of Famer

**While Yankee
Stadium was being
renovated from 1974
to 1976, the Yankees
shared Shea Stadium
with the Mets.**

Derek Jeter is the Yankees' current leader, both at the plate and in the field.

Roger Clemens. Manager Joe Torre has kept this
great assembly of talent moving in the right direction
since he took over in 1996.

Today's Yankees also now boast slugging third
baseman Alex Rodriguez. For Seattle and Texas,
"A-Rod" bashed 40 or more homers every year
from 1998 to 2003. The Yankees lost in the World
Series in 2001 and 2003, but remained among
baseball's top teams. It seems some things in baseball never change.

The Tampa Bay Devil Rays

The Tampa Bay Devil Rays were almost the Tampa Bay White Sox.

First, the Chicago White Sox had just about finalized plans to move to the Florida city in the late 1980s. However, Chicago city officials came up with the money to build the "Pale Hose" a new stadium, and the move never happened.

Then they were almost the Tampa Bay Mariners. The Seattle Mariners used the threat of moving to Florida to get their own new stadium funded. That left Tampa Bay still without a team!

In 1992, that team almost became the Tampa Bay Giants. Tampa businessman Vince Naimoli agreed to buy the San Francisco Giants and move them to his home city. But NL owners voted against the move—instead awarding Naimoli an **expansion team** in 1995. That team was named the Devil Rays, and they played

their first game in the new Tropicana Field on
March 31, 1998.

And that marked the high point of the franchise.
The following seasons provided few highlights.

Baseball has a long history in Florida. Since the
1920s, teams have traveled from the Northeast and
Midwest for spring training in the warm Sunshine
State. During spring training, teams get in shape for

Tampa's Tropicana Field became baseball's first home in South Florida in 1998.

the coming season and take a look at young players. They also play in what is called the Grapefruit League, facing other major league teams. Many fans plan vacations to Florida (or Arizona, where eight teams have spring training) to follow their favorites before the regular season starts.

With the addition of the Florida Marlins to the Miami area in 1993 and the Devil Rays in 1998, Florida now has two major league teams to go with the Grapefruit League. However, while the Marlins have brought two World Series trophies back home, the Devil Rays have not had any success.

Their first season featured a few bright spots. Rookie Rolando Arrojo won 14 games, the most ever by a pitcher on an expansion team. Outfielder Quinton McCracken set an expansion record with 179 hits.

A fan favorite was the addition of third baseman Wade Boggs to the first-year team. Boggs had grown up in the Tampa area and had been a star player in high school. With the Red Sox and Yankees in the big league, he had won five AL batting titles, earned 12 All-Star selections, and helped the Yankees win

Former batting champion Wade Boggs, a Tampa native, joined the new Devil Rays and achieved several career milestones.

Wilson Alvarez threw the first pitch in Devil Rays history. It was a ball, and the Devil Rays went on to lose 11–6.

First baseman Fred McGriff had his 400th career homer while with the Devil Rays in 2000.

the 1996 World Series. He joined the Devil Rays to close out his Hall of Fame career at home and hit the first homer in team history. In 1999, Boggs became the first player to make his 3,000th career hit a home run. He retired after the season ended.

There was another heartwarming story on the Devil Rays team that year. Relief pitcher Jim Morris made his major league debut for the team at the age of 35. He had been a high school coach for many years before his players urged him to try out. Morris discovered he had a stunning fastball, and his rise to the big league in only one year caught national attention. His tale was later made into the popular movie *The Rookie*, starring Dennis Quaid.

In 2000, the Devil Rays had something very odd happen. Though they play in a domed stadium, a game was postponed due to weather. Hurricane Gordon was raging, and the area was hit so hard by rain and wind that no one could get to the game! In 2001, the team reached 100 losses for the first time—not one of their favorite records.

For the 2003 season, Tampa Bay brought back another hometown favorite. Tampa native Lou Piniella was hired to manage the team. "Sweet Lou" had become an All-Star outfielder and star manager

Fiery manager Lou Piniella came home to Tampa to lead the Devil Rays.

(with Cincinnati and Seattle) after growing up in Tampa. Inspired by Piniella, and led by speedy outfielder Carl Crawford and slugging third baseman Aubrey Huff, the Devil Rays had one of their best seasons in 2004, winning 70 games. So the hope continues to grow for Devil Rays fans.

When tickets for the Devil Rays' first game went on sale in 1997, they sold out in 17 minutes!

The Toronto Blue Jays

Baseball has been a part of the Canadian sporting scene for more than 100 years. The first teams began play in the late 1800s. In 1874, a team from Ontario actually won the International League, a minor league one step below Major League Baseball. However, it was not until 1969 that Major League Baseball set up shop in the Great White North. That year, the Montreal Expos began play in the NL (though it was announced that they would leave in 2004).

The AL got its first Canadian team in 1977, when the Blue Jays began play in Toronto, Canada's largest city. The Blue Jays were added as an expansion team, joining the AL East.

Though Toronto's fans were excited to see the big leagues in their backyard for the first time, the team was disappointing on the field. It was not until 1983 that the team recorded its first winning season. Pitcher Dave Stieb was a bright spot for these early Jays teams. Stieb made the AL All-Star team five

Pitcher Dave Stieb was Toronto's ace on the way to its first AL East title in 1994.

times and posted five seasons with an earned run average (ERA) of 3.25 or lower.

After finishing second in 1984, the team won its first AL East title in 1985. Stieb led the league in ERAs, and lefty Jimmy Key won 14 games. The outfield trio of George Bell, Jesse Barfield, and Lloyd Moseby was one of the best in baseball, and all three hitters provided a ton of RBIs. However, the team lost in the ALCS to Kansas City.

Toronto played its first games in Exhibition Stadium.

George Bell of the Blue Jays was one of baseball's
most feared sluggers in the late 1980s.

The name *Blue Jays*
was chosen from
more than 4,000
entries in a Name
That Team contest
held in Toronto.

The 1987 season, though successful in some
ways, was a big disappointment. Key led the league
with a 2.76 ERA, and Bell's 134 RBIs helped him
win the AL MVP award. However, a seven-game
losing streak to end the season cost the Jays the

division crown. In 1988, Stieb continued the Jays'
"almost but not quite" streak. Twice he lost a
no-hitter with two outs in the ninth inning.

Manager Cito Gaston took over in 1989, and the
Jays won another division title. More importantly,
on June 5 of that year, the Jays moved into a new

**Manager Cito Gaston's leadership helped the Blue Jays
become two-time World Series champs.**

Dave Winfield hit this two-RBI double to help Toronto clinch its first title in 1992.

ballpark: the SkyDome. Still one of baseball's show-places, the SkyDome features a retractable roof, which means it can be pulled back along tracks to open the stadium to the sky. The outfield features a hotel in the stadium. Fans can rent rooms and watch games from their sofas! The great new park helped the Jays set a new AL attendance mark, as more than 3.4 millions fans poured in. By 1992, they had raised that mark above 4 million.

Another disappointing ALCS loss in 1991 spurred the Jays to bring in some **veteran** help for what would be a memorable 1992 season. Pitcher Jack Morris won 21 games, and future Hall of Famer Dave Winfield drove in 108 runs. The relief duo of Tom Henke and Duane Ward were key to Toronto's victory over Oakland in the ALCS. The World Series, for the first time, was coming to Canada!

In the series, the Jays' deep pitching staff helped the team hold off the powerful Atlanta Braves. In six games, Toronto became the first team from outside the United States to be World Series champions.

In 1993, the team kept their streak going. John Olerud, Paul Molitor, and Roberto Alomar finished 1-2-3 in the AL batting race. That was the first time that had happened in the 20th century. Toronto's

Joe Carter's series-winning homer in 1993 was the second ever. Pittsburgh's Bill Mazeroski won the 1960 series with a ninth-inning solo shot.

Time to celebrate! Joe Carter leaps for joy after hitting a series-winning homer in 1993.

After several near-misses, Dave Stieb finally became the first Toronto pitcher with a no-hitter in 1990.

World Series battle against the Philadelphia Phillies provided two important highlights. The first came in Game 4, when the Jays outlasted the Phils 15–14 in the highest-scoring World Series game ever. The second was one for the ages. In Game 6, with the Jays trailing 6–5 in the ninth inning, Joe Carter hit a two-out, three-run home run that gave Toronto the game and its second straight series title. Carter's joyous leaping around the bases is part of baseball's all-time highlight reel.

While Toronto has not been to the playoffs again since 1993, there were some memorable moments.

Pitcher Pat Hentgen won the 1996 AL Cy Young Award. Former Boston ace Roger Clemens won two straight Cy Young Awards in 1997 and 1998. In 2000, the team became the second in history to have seven players with 20 or more homers. In 2003, first baseman Carlos Delgado led the majors with 145 RBIs.

In their short history, the Blue Jays have made quite an impression on their neighbors to the south.

Third baseman Eric Hinske was the 2002 AL Rookie of the Year.

First baseman Carlos Delgado specializes in long homers and clutch RBIs.

TEAM RECORDS (THROUGH 2004)

Team	All-time Record	World Series Titles (Most Recent)	Number of Times in the Postseason	Top Manager (Wins)
Baltimore*	7,668–8,399	3 (1983)	11	Earl Weaver (1,480)
Boston	8,263–7,817	6 (2004)	16	Joe Cronin (1,071)
New York**	9,097–6,962	26 (2000)	44	Joe McCarthy (1,460)
Tampa Bay	451–680	0	0	Larry Rothschild (205)
Toronto	2,178–2,233	2 (1993)	5	Cito Gaston (683)

includes Milwaukee and St. Louis
**includes Baltimore*

AMERICAN LEAGUE EAST
CAREER LEADERS (THROUGH 2004)

Baltimore

Category	Name (Years with Team)	Total
Batting Average	Heinie Manush (1928–1930)	.362
Home Runs	Cal Ripken Jr. (1981–2001)	431
RBI	Cal Ripken Jr. (1981–2001)	1,695
Stolen Bases	George Sisler (1915–1927)	351
Wins	Jim Palmer (1965–1984)	268
Saves	Gregg Olson (1988–1993)	160
Strikeouts	Jim Palmer (1965–1984)	2,212

AMERICAN LEAGUE EAST CAREER LEADERS (THROUGH 2004)

Boston

Category	Name (Years with Team)	Total
Batting Average	Ted Williams (1939–1942, 1946–1960)	.344
Home Runs	Ted Williams (1939–1942, 1946–1960)	521
RBI	Carl Yastrzemski (1961–1983)	1,844
Stolen Bases	Harry Hooper (1909–1920)	300
Wins	Roger Clemens (1984–1996)	192
	Cy Young (1901–08)	192
Saves	Bob Stanley (1977–1989)	132
Strikeouts	Roger Clemens (1984–1996)	2,590

New York

Category	Name (Years with Team)	Total
Batting Average	Babe Ruth (1920–1934)	.349
Home Runs	Babe Ruth (1920–1934)	659
RBI	Lou Gehrig (1923–1939)	1,995
Stolen Bases	Rickey Henderson (1985–89)	326
Wins	Whitey Ford (1950, 1953–1967)	236
Saves	Mariano Rivera (1995–2004)	336
Strikeouts	Whitey Ford (1950, 1953–1967)	1,956

AMERICAN LEAGUE EAST CAREER LEADERS (THROUGH 2004)

Tampa Bay

Category	Name (Years with Team)	Total
Batting Average	Aubrey Huff (2000–04)	.295
Home Runs	Fred McGriff (1998–2001, 2004)	99
RBI	Fred McGriff (1998–2001, 2004)	359
Stolen Bases	Carl Crawford (2002–04)	123
Wins	Victor Zambrano (2001–04)	35
Saves	Roberto Hernandez (1998–2000)	101
Strikeouts	Victor Zambrano (2001–04)	372

Toronto

Category	Name (Years with Team)	Total
Batting Average	Roberto Alomar (1991–95)	.307
Home Runs	Carlos Delgado (1993–2004)	336
RBI	Carlos Delgado (1993–2004)	1,058
Stolen Bases	Lloyd Moseby (1980–89)	255
Wins	Dave Stieb (1979–1992, 1998)	175
Saves	Tom Henke (1985–1992)	217
Strikeouts	Dave Stieb (1979–1992, 1998)	1,658

Glossary

brash—energetic and seemingly overconfident

closer—a relief pitcher brought in at the end of a game to save a victory

Cy Young Award—the award annually given to the best pitcher in each league

expansion team—a new franchise that starts from scratch, thus increasing (or expanding) the total number of clubs in a given league

Green Monster—nickname for the large left-field wall at Boston's Fenway Park

Lou Gehrig's disease—nickname for amyotrophic lateral sclerosis (ALS), an often fatal nerve disease

no-hitter—a complete game in which the pitcher or pitchers for one team do not allow the opposing team any hits

ovation—loud and long applause or cheering by a crowd to show approval

pennant—the championship of each league (American and National)

postseason—the playoffs, which start with the Division Series, continue with the League Championship Series, and conclude with the World Series

switch-hitter—a player who can bat from both the left and right sides of the plate

traditions—elements passed down from generation to generation (or from team to team)

Triple Crown—for a hitter, it means leading the league in batting average, home runs, and RBIs in the same season; less often, it refers to a pitcher who leads the league in wins, strikeouts, and ERAs in the same season

veteran—a player who has been in the game for many years

wild card—a team that finishes in second place in its division but still makes the playoffs

World Series—baseball's championship event; the winners of the AL and NL pennants annually meet in a best-of-seven series to determine the world champion

Time Line

1901   Boston joins the AL as one of the league's first teams.

1915   Boston wins the first of three World Series titles in four seasons.

1920   Babe Ruth joins the Yankees from the Red Sox, turning the "Bronx Bombers" into a powerhouse.

1936   The Yankees win their first of four straight World Series titles.

1939   Lou Gehrig of the Yankees retires due to the illness that will take his life. Gehrig played in a record 2,130 consecutive games.

1953   The Yankees win their fifth straight World Series, the most consecutive championships in baseball history.

1954   The St. Louis Browns move to Baltimore and become the Orioles.

1966   Baltimore wins the World Series over the Dodgers.

1970   Baltimore wins the World Series over the Reds.

1983   Baltimore wins the World Series over the Phillies.

1992   Toronto becomes the first Canadian team to win the World Series; they win again in 1993.

1995   Cal Ripken Jr. of the Orioles breaks Lou Gehrig's consecutive games-played streak.

1996   Yankees win their first World Series since 1978; it's their record 23rd title all-time.

1998   Tampa Bay Devil Rays begin play in the AL East.

2000   Yankees become the first team since the 1974 Oakland Athletics to win three World Series in a row.

2004   Boston sweeps the Cardinals in the World Series for their first championship since 1918.

For More Information

BOOKS

Gutman, Dan. *Babe & Me: A Baseball Card Adventure.* New York: Avon Books, 2000.

McCormack, Shaun. *Ted Williams.* New York: Rosen Central, 2004.

Nichols, John. *The History of the Tampa Bay Devil Rays.* Mankato, Minn.: Creative Education, 2000.

Young, Robert. *A Personal Tour of Camden Yards.* Minneapolis: Lerner Publications Company, 1999.

ON THE WEB

Visit our home page for lots of links about the American League East teams: *http://www.childsworld.com/links.html*

Note to Parents, Teachers, and Librarians: We routinely check our Web links to make sure they're safe, active sites—so encourage your readers to check them out!

Index

ABOUT THE AUTHOR

James Buckley Jr. has written more than 35 books on sports for young readers, including titles about baseball, football, hockey, soccer, and the Olympics. His other baseball books for kids include *Eyewitness Baseball*, *The Visual Dictionary of Baseball*, *Super Shortstops*, *Strikeout Kings*, and *Play Ball: The Official Major League Baseball Guide for Young Players*.